Joy

To my five sons, fearless and beyond reproach!
G. T.

To my children and my godchildren.
V. M.

To all the children I coach in managing their emotions.
S. d. N.

Under the direction of Romain Lizé, CEO, MAGNIFICAT
Editor, MAGNIFICAT: Isabelle Galmiche
Editor, Ignatius: Vivian Dudro
Translator: Janet Chevrier
Proofreader: Kathleen Hollenbeck
Graphic Designers: Armelle Riva, Thérèse Jauze
Layout: Gauthier Delauné
Production: Thierry Dubus, Audrey Bord

Original French edition: *Trop de Joie!*
© 2018 by Mame, Paris
© 2021 by MAGNIFICAT, New York • Ignatius Press, San Francisco
ISBN MAGNIFICAT 978-1-63967-011-6 • ISBN Ignatius Press 978-1-62164-602-0

how to HANDLE MY EMOTIONS

Joy

~~~~~~~~~~~~~~~~~~~~

THREE STORIES ABOUT SHARING JOY

~~~~~~~~~~~~~~~~~~~~

Gaëlle Tertrais • Violaine Moulière • Ségolène de Noüel
Caroline Modeste

Magnificat · Ignatius

Contents

Introduction

Joy is a wonderful emotion! Unlike fear or anger, it is a pleasant emotion, so you may wonder why you would ever need help handling it. Yet, depending on what you do with joy, it can either open your heart to others or cause you to focus only on yourself.

In these stories, you will learn how to recognize the emotion of joy: when you wear a smile from ear to ear, when you feel like jumping about and singing at the top of your lungs, and when everything around you seems beautiful. You will learn how to share your joy, how to share it with tact, and how to persevere when difficulties arise.

God is the source of our joy, and he wants us to experience all the benefits this emotion can bring.

In each story, through the little pictures in the margin, you will accompany Elliot and Charlotte as they progress through their experiences of joy, and discover the entire toolbox of virtues they are using to make the most of it.

1

A Box of Chocolates

"Charlo-o-o?! The postman is here with a package for you!"

"Yippee! What fun! A package just for me!"

Charlotte didn't need to be asked twice: she took the stairs two by two, rushing to get to the front door. Her heart felt as though it skipped a beat. "A package!" she thought. "How exciting!"

CHARLOTTE NOTICES HOW HER BODY IS REACTING.

Charlotte's mom handed her a round box wrapped in a pretty gold paper. On the outside were Christmas postage stamps. "Hmm," thought Charlotte, looking at the address. "I've seen that handwriting before. This is a present from Uncle Max!"

Once Charlotte ripped off the wrapping, she surveyed with delight an entire box of chocolates. Inside, the pieces were neatly arranged in rows—milk chocolates and dark chocolates with yummy fillings.

"Oh, can I try one?" asked her little brother, Norbert, reaching his hand out to take a piece.

"No! They're mine!" shouted Charlotte, snapping the lid back on the box.

She rushed back into her room as her brother yelled after her: "Selfish!"

But Charlotte didn't care; these chocolates were hers! She wasn't about to let him spoil her joy!

Comfortably seated on her bed, Charlotte was ready to savor the chocolates all by herself. To start with, she chose one wrapped in pretty silver paper. She unwrapped it and felt the chocolate shell crunch between her teeth. Then a praline cream melted in her mouth. Mmm... it was so-o-o good! She picked out another one covered in hazelnut chips and ate it in one bite. She gave a deep sigh of contentment. How good it tasted...

The chocolates disappeared into her mouth, one after the other.

The rows became shorter and shorter. Charlotte knew she should stop, but instead she thought, "Just one more." And after she ate that chocolate, she said to herself, "Well, this one with pistachios will be my last piece."

All at once, Charlotte realized she had gone too far. She started to feel queasy. Her joy gave way to a tummy ache. She was forced to lie still for a while until her stomach settled down. In time she sat up and leaned her cheek against the frosty window by her bed. Then she spotted the little house of Auntie Ivy, her elderly neighbor. That gave her an idea!

"Auntie Ivy will help me feel better!" thought Charlotte. Quickly hiding her chocolate box under her pillow (just in case Norbert came looking for it), she put on her winter coat and went outside.

Auntie Ivy opened her door with a big smile. "Come in quickly, my dear! Brrr, it's so cold out!"

While Charlotte warmed herself by the radiator, Auntie Ivy gaily busied herself. She hummed as she pasted labels on the jam jars she had prepared last summer: "Strawberry Surprise," "Apricot Delight," and "Blueberry Bliss." Then she tied them up in silk ribbons. Her jam jars had been transformed into pretty little packages.

Charlotte asked her, "Why are you wrapping those up? Aren't you going to eat them?"

"No, my dear," Auntie Ivy replied. "I'm going to give them away!"

"Really? But to whom?" Charlotte asked.

"Ah well, that will be a bit of a surprise even for me. I'll give them to whomever I happen to meet tonight."

"No! Really?" Charlotte thought to herself, stunned. "Auntie Ivy was going to give away these delicious jars of jam to total strangers? What a crazy idea!"

Auntie Ivy saw that Charlotte didn't understand, so she tried to explain.

"Sharing with others when you don't have to, that's what it means to be generous," she said. "And generosity brings happiness to both those who give and those who receive."

"Well, okay, those who receive—I understand their joy," Charlotte agreed. "But those who give? I don't see how that can make them happy when it means less for themselves."

Auntie Ivy smiled and her eyes sparkled.

"It's true that at first it's hard not to keep everything for yourself," she said. "But once you begin sharing, you realize you're richer than before. Your heart grows bigger!"

Charlotte thought of the chocolates she had wanted to keep for herself.

Auntie Ivy's voice interrupted her thoughts. "I'm all set," she said. "Would you like to come with me?"

"Oh, yes!" exclaimed Charlotte. "I want to see this!"

Back outside, Charlotte helped Auntie Ivy pull her shopping cart with the jam jars tucked safely in place. Darkness had fallen, and the cold stung their noses, but how delightful it was to stroll among the bright, festive decorations! Everything looked and smelled like Christmas! Charlotte's heart once again filled with joy.

Charlotte and Auntie Ivy came upon a beggar shivering in the street. Auntie Ivy suddenly stopped, rummaged in her cart, and placed one of her jam jars into the hands of this poor man. A big smile lit up his face, and he bobbed his head in thanks! Charlotte was pleased to see this, and she smiled back at him.

Just like that, her little old neighbor was already off down the street. Charlotte caught up with her, and they walked on to the corner supermarket, where each cashier received a little jar of jam. They hardly had time to thank Auntie Ivy before she was off again!

Back on the sidewalk, Charlotte walked straight into Elliot, who was just stepping out from his guitar lesson.

"What are you doing here, Charlo?" he asked in surprise.

"I'm keeping Auntie Ivy company," Charlotte replied, reaching into the cart. "Here," she said, offering Elliot a little jar of jam. "That's for you!"

"Oh, uh, that's... that's cool!" Elliot beamed. "Thank you!"

Charlotte and Ivy continued their little tour of the neighborhood until, little by little, the shopping cart was nearly empty. The two friends offered their last gifts to a mother and her three children. The woman looked quite tired after a hard day, but then the same miracle happened again: a chilly winter face lit up with a sunny smile.

The chimes of the town clock signaled that it was dinnertime. Before running off, Charlotte hugged Auntie Ivy and told her how much she had enjoyed their adventure.

CHARLOTTE RECOGNIZES HER NEED TO SPREAD HER JOY!

"Giving away all that jam was so much fun!" thought Charlotte. "I wish it could go on forever!"

Back in her bedroom, Charlotte started to think.

CHARLOTTE STOPS TO THINK.

She pulled the box of chocolates from under her pillow and realized she had the choice of keeping the rest for herself or sharing them. She longed to eat them all then and there, but something within her had changed: she felt that by sharing them, her joy would increase.

To be generous—that's what she wanted!

CHARLOTTE CHOOSES THE VIRTUE OF GENEROSITY.

To give herself courage, she stretched out her arms and opened her hands. "You can't give with closed fists," she thought, smiling.

Charlotte wrapped up all the remaining chocolates in gold paper and ribbons!

She then slipped quietly into each bedroom, looking for the best place to put her chocolates: one on Dad's pillow, one on Mom's book, another in her little brother's sneakers, and one next to Annie's stuffed panda.

She had one more chocolate left. Where could she put it? As she considered eating it, Charlotte opened her other hand and remembered her generous neighbor. "Auntie Ivy! That's it!" she thought, all excited.

With her wool hat down over her ears and a scarf wrapped around her nose, Charlotte set out. Guided by the glimmer of the streetlights, she placed her last chocolate on Auntie Ivy's doorstep. She rang the doorbell and crouched in the shadows, eager to see what would happen. Auntie Ivy opened the door and searched the darkness to see who had rung. Then she spotted it, right at her feet: the piece of chocolate from Charlotte. She carefully gathered it up and unwrapped it. Then, with eyes closed, she chewed it slowly with an enormous smile on her face!

Charlotte's heart overflowed with a joy much bigger and much deeper than before! She felt as if she had wings. Still lost in thought as she

returned home. She was surprised to find Mom, Dad, Annie, and Norbert bubbling with happiness in the front hall. They gave her big hugs and showered her with thanks for her chocolates. Even little Norbert said his sister was the best!

Thanks to Uncle Max and Auntie Ivy, Charlotte learned that there is more joy in giving than in receiving. And she now knew how to handle the joy of getting good things: with open hands.

Charlotte learned to use the virtue of generosity (the little sister of justice), which means freely sharing with those around you—not just when you must.

2

The Birthday Party

Elliot couldn't sit still. His birthday was coming soon! He wanted to celebrate with an amusement park right at home. There would be an inflatable pool filled with bouncy balls in the yard, a giant slide down the stairs, and, in the attic, an obstacle course between elastic ropes. There would be music. And all his friends would be invited: Tim, Jack, Oliver, and Charlotte!

He couldn't wait. If only he could make time go faster! He had butterflies in his stomach and ants in his pants; he hopped; he twirled; he jumped for joy.

ELLIOT NOTICES HOW HIS BODY IS REACTING.

23

All day long, Dad kept telling him to calm down. "Elliot, you won't make your birthday come any quicker by jumping around like that!" he said.

"My birthday! Yippee!" Elliot shouted, bouncing up and down on the living room couch. Dad rolled his eyes.

ELLIOT OWNS HIS EMOTION.

Elliot replied, "I can't help it, Dad! I have so much joy inside!"

The next day at school, Elliot announced the big news to his friends and handed out invitations. His schoolmates gathered around him like bees buzzing around honey. All excited, he told them about the activities he planned to have.

"You'll see, the giant slide will be amazing! We'll land on cushions at the bottom."

Everyone broke out in oohs and aahs.

Elliot could hardly contain his joy. It was like a volcano just waiting to explode.

He spoke louder and louder, he was shaking, and he rocked with laughter! But his laughter came to an abrupt halt with a poke in his ribs from Charlotte.

"Ow! That hurt!" he shouted.

"Elliot, you didn't invite Sacha," she whispered with a frown.

And there he was, Sacha, right in front of Elliot, looking sad. Sacha was in a wheelchair; his movements were always a bit slow. At school, a lady helped him with his work. He was nice, and Elliot really liked him. But, since this was about his birthday, he whispered back to Charlotte:

"I can't invite him! He won't be able to do anything in a wheelchair!"

"Maybe," Charlotte answered in a hushed voice, "but if you can't invite him, at least stop talking about it right in front of him. That's impolite! It's not tactful."

Immediately, Elliot felt his bubble burst.

That evening during supper, Elliot was feeling sad. Suddenly, he asked his mother: "Mom, what exactly does 'tactful' mean?"

His mom raised her eyebrows in surprise. "Why do you ask me that?" she said.

"Because of Sacha," Elliot explained. "Charlotte told me it wasn't tactful of me to talk about my birthday party in front of him."

"Ah... why? Didn't you invite him?" his mom asked.

"Well, uh... no," Elliot answered.

"So he saw you all being happy together without including him?" she continued.

"I guess so." Elliot sighed deeply.

"And how do you think he felt about that?"

"Um... he looked sad. But, Mom, I promise, I didn't mean to be unkind. I was just so super happy! I didn't notice."

ELLIOT RECOGNIZES HIS NEED TO SHARE HIS JOY WITH HIS FRIENDS.

"I know," his mom replied. "But that's just what it means to be tactful: to think of other people's feelings before saying something."

Elliot was beginning to understand. The volcano of joy within him had exploded all over Sacha. It wasn't nice of him.

"Does that mean I should pretend not to be joyful, then?" he asked.

"Of course not!" his mom replied, stroking his hair. "Stay joyful. But you could try to restrain it a little to avoid hurting those around you."

To show him how to do that, breathing softly, his mom lowered her two hands. And, following her example, Elliot managed to lower the power of that volcano within him.

"Whenever you feel that joy boiling over," she told him, "take a deep breath and make this gesture. That will help you to be tactful."

Elliot thought about it.

ELLIOT THINKS.

27

ELLIOT CHOOSES THE VIRTUE OF TACTFULNESS.

ELLIOT CHOSE A TOOL: HE BREATHED SLOWLY AS HE LOWERED HIS HANDS.

Elliot overflowed with joy at the thought of his coming birthday, but he had not meant to hurt Sacha's feelings. He liked Sacha and wanted to be nice to him. So, from now on, Elliot would try to be tactful!

He breathed slowly as he lowered his hands and quietly whispered: "Tactful, Elliot. Be tactful..."

Elliot tossed and turned in bed all night. He felt bad whenever he remembered Sacha. "It would be great if he could come to the party too," he thought. Then it dawned on him. He would take care of this first thing tomorrow!

The next morning, Elliot rushed to school with one last invitation in his hand. He hurried to offer it to Sacha, who opened it with wide-eyed surprise.

"Is this really for me?" Sacha asked.

Elliot nodded and smiled at him. Sacha's eyes glowed with delight. He was so happy! In his heart, Elliot felt a flood of joy like never before. He gave a great big laugh. How good it felt to be considerate of others!

On the day of Elliot's birthday, amidst his friends in the garden, Sacha helped decorate his wheelchair with colored balloons. He laughed and clapped his hands, his face glowing with happiness.

"Let the games commence!" Elliot said. "First, the Smell Detective."

Elliot was overexcited: he wanted to be the first to play! But he felt his joy boiling over and remembered what his mom had told him. So he quietly stepped aside, took a deep breath, and lowered his hands, saying to himself, "Tactful, Elliot. Be tactful..."

ELLIOT PUTS THE VIRTUE OF TACTFULNESS INTO PRACTICE.

Then he turned around to Sacha: "You first!"

With his eyes masked, Sacha sniffed the pots one by one: mustard, strawberry jam, cinnamon, and toothpaste. He got them all right.

"Well done, Sacha!" Elliot clapped. Not one of the next contestants did as well.

"Tee-hee," Sacha giggled. "I may not be able to walk, but I've got a great nose!"

The games went on all day: Blind Man's Bluff, darts, and others. Without a word, Elliot decided to cancel the slide down the stairway; Sacha could never take part in that. A bit disappointed, he took a slow breath and repeated: "Tactful, Elliot. Be tactful..." And he ended the afternoon with a game of two-person flag football.

Wow, Sacha was great in offense! Sacha caught the ball hiked to him by Elliot and managed to score! Everyone cheered: "Way to go, Sacha!" They all gathered around him to give him a high-five! All of the friends were bursting with joy.

"One for all and all for one," they cheered.

Elliot was delighted. This was his best birthday ever! Now that he was trying to be tactful, his joy just grew and grew.

To avoid offending Sacha with his boundless joy, Elliot used tact (the little sister of temperance), which means being thoughtful of others and tempering one's behavior.

The Bike Ride

"Ya-hooo!! I'm flying!" screamed Charlotte as she zoomed downhill with the wind in her hair and stars in her eyes. Right behind her, Elliot gave a shout of joy.

"This is so great!"

They arrived at the bottom of the hill completely out of breath and their hair tangled. As soon as they finally came to a halt, they broke into laughter. What a descent on their bikes; it was insane! Charlotte felt her heart beating like a drum.

They had left both sets of parents and Norbert, Archie, and Annie behind, eating their dust! Elliot and Charlotte took advantage of the moment to take a breather.

Charlotte leaned her bike against a tree. Short of breath and with her cheeks still stinging from the speed and the wind, she lay down on the green grass. She closed her eyes. Stretched out on the ground with the warm earth beneath her, she became aware of the tiniest sounds: her rapid breathing, the crickets' singing, the rustling of leaves in the breeze, and the rumbling of a distant plane. She felt the heat of the sun on her face. Oh, how good it was! A great feeling of well-being filled her heart.

CHARLOTTE NOTICES HOW HER BODY IS REACTING.

Turning to Elliot, she said, "Today's bike ride was so wonderful! Let's never let anything spoil it. You agree, Elliot? You promise?"

"I promise," he replied. "Not anything ever! It will always remain a super day!"

With a huge smile on her lips, Charlotte laid her head back down on the grass. The sky was so blue. What a wonderful world!

How was it possible to feel so happy?

CHARLOTTE OWNS HER EMOTION.

Suddenly, a shout woke her from her thoughts. "Yoo-hoo!"

There were the others. They looked a bit tired. But they arrived at just the right moment. It was time for a snack. They all sat down in a circle on the grass.

"Oof," said Archie, his face as red as a beet. "I couldn't go any farther."

He pulled out his water bottle and glugged down great gulps. Suddenly, Charlotte felt a plop of water on her forehead.

"Oh, Archie, watch out! You're splashing me!" she yelled.

"That wasn't me!"

Charlotte raised her eyes and saw that the beautiful blue sky of a moment ago was growing dark with storm clouds.

"Uh-oh! The weather's turned," said Charlotte's dad. "It's time to think of going home!"

With that, the downpour began. They raced to wrap up the food they had barely tasted.

"But, but, but! I haven't had my snack yet!" Archie yelled.

As they rushed about, even Charlotte's mom moaned and groaned a bit.

"Come on, everyone, hurry up!" said Elliot's dad. "We need to get home as fast as we can!"

Elliot pouted, a dark look on his face. This wonderful day was turning into a fiasco. Some of them were already drenched, and a bad mood had taken hold.

How foolish to let a little rain ruin such a great day! thought Charlotte. They had promised not to let anything spoil it!

CHARLOTTE
RECOGNIZES
HER NEED:
TO ENJOY
A GOOD DAY.

Charlotte shot a quick look at Elliot. He looked so pathetic, with his soaked hair and raindrops running down his neck, that she broke out in laughter. "It's not the end of the world!" she said.

Elliot tried to look annoyed, but on hearing her giggle, he too broke out in laughter.

Charlotte considered:

CHARLOTTE
THINKS.

Things hadn't gone the way she had hoped. But nothing could be done about that. So, why complain all day long? That wouldn't solve anything. No! Chin up! Soaked from head to foot, Charlotte decided to maintain her good mood!

CHARLOTTE
CHOOSES
THE VIRTUE
OF PERSEVERANCE.

She wondered if a smile might help her and the others to feel better.

She turned to Elliot and said: "You know, Elliot, whatever happens, it'll still be a great day! I promise!"

Then she unleashed her greatest asset: she smiled from ear to ear.

CHARLOTTE
CHOSE A TOOL:
A SMILE.

"Come on, Elliot, try smiling. It will make you feel better."

A bigger and bigger smile spread over Elliot's dripping-wet face.

The next moment they were off again! With good humor as their engine, they got back on their bikes and followed the others, who were already pedaling away. Elliot and Charlotte over-took all of them, cycling like mad and singing like crazy. Charlotte smiled at the clouds.

CHARLOTTE
PRACTICES
THE VIRTUE OF
PERSEVERANCE.

The rain beat down on Charlotte's face. She opened her mouth wide open, stuck out her tongue, and drank down the big raindrops. The water was cool. How lovely it was, this summer rain!

Just a few yards ahead, a huge puddle stretched before them, right in the middle of the road.

"Do you see that?" Elliot asked her, his eyes bright with mischief.

"Yep! You ready?" Charlotte replied with a laugh.

"Let's go!" They both yelled.

Whoosh! They pedaled straight through the puddle, chilly water splashing all around them. Behind them, Norbert and Archie also set off into the puddle amid great bursts of laughter.

"Be careful!" Charlotte's mom shouted.

Charlotte spotted her dad also splashing through the water.

"I can't believe it!" she said, laughing.

Then Elliot's parents did the same. With each puddle, they tried to see who could splash the most. Charlotte's mom began competing too.

Annie clapped her hands, shouting: "Again! Again! Another splash in the water!"

That evening, they all arrived at Charlotte's house soaking wet. Their shoes squished as they walked.

"Who'd like some sock juice?" Elliot shouted as he emptied his sopping wet sneaker right in front of Charlotte's nose. To get him back, she squeezed her wet pigtail over his head. They laughed until their sides hurt!

"Come warm yourselves up in the kitchen!"
Charlotte's mom said. Then, she whispered into
her daughter's ear: "Thank you, Charlo, for keeping a good sense of humor despite everything.
That's what I call perseverance!"

Soon, the two families were gathered around
the table with mugs of steaming hot chocolate
and a snack. Everyone had pink cheeks and a
broad smile.

Wet socks were drying all over the radiators. They gave off a funny smell, but Charlotte didn't care. She leaned close to Elliot and whispered in his ear, "That promise we made paid off! We had a super day!"

"Yeah," he said with a grin. "That was so much fun!"

At the window, Charlotte watched the rain fall and smiled. She had made a great discovery today: no dark clouds or thunderstorms could take away her joy.

When you run into difficulties, look on the bright side like Charlotte, who chose to keep her good humor!

To keep her joy, Charlotte made use of the virtue of perseverance (the little sister of fortitude), which means not giving up when difficulties arise.

WHAT HAVE YOU LEARNED FROM THESE STORIES?

JOY IS
(Check the right answer.)

☐ A good emotion
☐ A pleasant emotion
☐ An unpleasant emotion

There is no good or bad emotion. Every emotion sends us a message. But, of course, joy is a pleasant emotion!

JOY ACCOMPANIES THE FULFILLMENT OF CERTAIN NEEDS. WHICH ONES?
(Number these in their order of importance to you.)

☐ To be happy with one another
☐ To succeed at something
☐ To feel loved
☐ To do things we enjoy
☐ To love one another just as we are
☐ To contemplate beautiful things

HOW DO ELLIOT AND CHARLOTTE DEAL WITH THEIR JOY?
In each story, two options are open to them.
(Fill in the virtuous path.)

1 Charlotte could enjoy her chocolates on her own, but she chose

2 Elliot's joy at his coming birthday party could make others uncomfortable, but he chose

3 Charlotte and Elliot could have lost their joy when the rain began, but they chose

WHAT HAPPENS IF I DON'T SHARE MY JOY?
(Check all that apply.)

☐ I remain focused on myself.
☐ My joy diminishes little by little.
☐ I isolate myself from others.
☐ I no longer notice or appreciate other joys.

VIRTUES COME TO THE AID OF EMOTIONS!

In each story, to share their joy with others, Elliot and Charlotte chose a virtue.

Do you know what a virtue is? A virtue is the habit of choosing to do what is right. At first, that takes effort. But with time, it becomes easier and easier... a little like learning to ride a bicycle!

SPOTLIGHT ON THE VIRTUE OF JUSTICE

"That's not fair!" That's something you often repeat when something seems unfair: when you have to go to bed but your brother gets to stay up later, when you're punished instead of someone else, when someone breaks a promise, and so on. How can you decide who is right and if the situation is really unfair? Well, the virtue of justice is there **to help you give everyone his due**: to give food to those who are hungry, to obey rules and restrictions, to keep your promises...

The more you practice the virtue of justice, the more you become not only more just yourself but also more able to recognize real injustices and develop the desire to correct them.

Do you know any sayings about joy? *"Happy as a lark"* or *"I'm on cloud nine"* are two. Can you think of two others?

Since it's not always easy to practice the virtues, Elliot and Charlotte find tools to help them!

Find these tools in the stories and link them below to the corresponding virtues.

Virtue of generosity •

Virtue of tactfulness •

Virtue of perseverance •

• CHARLOTTE AND ELLIOT CHOOSE TO SMILE WHEN FACED WITH DIFFICULTIES.

• CHARLOTTE OPENS HER HANDS IN ORDER TO SHARE.

• ELLIOT BREATHES AS HE LOWERS HIS HANDS AND REPEATS: "TACTFUL, ELLIOT. BE TACTFUL."

THE PATHWAY THROUGH EMOTIONS

An emotion is a reaction to an event perceived by our five senses. It tells us we need something. Then it's up to us to work through it! To better understand what's happening, follow Elliot and Charlotte along the pathway of emotions!

I OWN MY EMOTION.

I ACT

So now, how do I deal with my emotion? Let's break it down into steps.

1. EXPERIENCING A STIMULUS
I have a positive experience involving other people or my surroundings.

2. SENSING MY EMOTIONAL REACTION
I sense: lightheartedness, the smile on my face.
I feel: relaxation, strength, awe at the beauty before me.

3. IDENTIFYING THE EMOTION
I ask myself: What am I feeling?
I realize: I feel joy.

4. OWNING THE EMOTION
I own the emotion for what it is: an emotion itself is neither good nor bad.

HOW WILL I HAN
MY EMOTION?

8. MAKING A DECISION

choose how to react:
o share, to be attentive to others, not to give up.

9. TAKING ACTION

use the tools that will help me exercise virtue:
open up my hands, lower them down as I
breathe slowly, and smile.

10. PRACTICING DAY AFTER DAY

10

9

8

6

5

TEMPTATION

REGRET

HAPPINESS
Love, peace,
joy, respect, self-
esteem, and so on.

UNHAPPINESS
Closing in on myself,
being insensitive to
others, giving up too
soon, and so on.

I STOP TO THINK...

How will I handle my emotion?

5. DISCERNING WHAT TO DO
I think about what would be good for me
and others.

6. RECOGNIZING WHAT I NEED
I need to share, to celebrate,
to open myself up to others.

7. SEEKING WAYS TO ANSWER MY NEED
VIRTUES/VICES
Generosity, tactfulness, perseverance.
Greediness, tactlessness, moodiness.

VICE OR VIRTUE?

From their earliest years, children are able to identify specific emotions, and from the age of reason, they have the capacity to deal with them. This unique series on the emotions responds to that potential with both faith and guidance, offering a virtuous pathway to a happy life.

Joy is a highly valued and sought-after emotion. We get out of bed every morning in the hope of happiness. Joy is a feeling of exultation that makes us feel strong. It's a sign that we are in harmony with our surroundings, that our hopes and desires will come to fruition.

AS A PARENT, TEACHER, OR EDUCATOR, HOW DO YOU TEACH JOY TO CHILDREN?

First of all, be open to the causes of joy. We have five senses that enable us to be receptive to our surroundings. Take time to encourage the child to pay attention to the signals our bodies send to make us aware of good, pleasant, and beautiful things all around us:

➡ Through sight—the loveliness of the countryside, the kindness of a smiling face...

➡ Through smell—the aroma of freshly baked bread, the scent of a flower...

➡ Through hearing—the sound of music, the song of birds...

➡ Through taste—the sweetness of caramel, the spiciness of cinnamon...

➡ Through touch—the warmth of sunshine, the comfort of a hug...

Once we are aware of the causes of joy around us, we can experience wonder and gratitude, which are sisters of joy.

Don't forget:

Knowing how to identify
something as good, pleasant,
or beautiful leads to joy.

Transform This Test through the Virtues

Your five senses allow you to appreciate each moment of joy. And these little moments of joy added to one another contribute to a happy state of mind, giving you high spirits.

• Like Charlotte and Elliot, you can transform a short moment of joy into true happiness thanks to the virtues of generosity, tactfulness, and perseverance, which open you to others. Your joy will increase as it spills over to others; it will never run out. **That's how joy enters the virtuous pathway.** It then goes beyond being a pleasant emotion and fills your heart.

• On the other hand, when you seek pleasure solely for yourself, without sharing it, you may momentarily feel happy, but your heart remains empty. And so you seek more, but in vain. **This endless search for pleasure leads to greediness, which is a vice**, the opposite of virtue. Greediness makes us more and more dependent on pleasure, which little by little isolates us and can even lead us to use others to satisfy our desires. That will make us unhappy, for we are made for relationships, to love and be loved.

Joy expands our hearts and opens us up to sharing. It radiates out to others. Joy encourages us to hug, to celebrate, to share, to give, and to welcome others!

However, sometimes, joy can lead to self-absorption, which distances us from those around us or from the situation we are in. That's what happens when there is **too much** joy combined with a focus on ourselves.

AS A PARENT, A TEACHER, OR AN EDUCATOR, HOW CAN YOU EXPLAIN THIS TO A CHILD?

• Offer your full attention.

As soon as you notice that your child's joy is becoming excessive, stop what you and your child are doing. Stoop down to your child's level. Firmly and with a smile, indicate that you want to talk with him or her privately.

• Listen.

Encourage the child to verbalize what he or she is feeling and to name the emotion. If need be, ask a few questions: "Are you thrilled?" "Are you wild with joy?" "Are you feeling over the moon?" If the child is speaking loudly and making wild gestures to unleash joy, don't hesitate to allow the child to express himself or herself. The joy is legitimate—it's what he or she is feeling. Don't judge the child even if the child is going a bit too far.

Take the child's hands in yours or place your hands on his or her shoulders to help the child settle down. Don't talk. And avoid words like "Calm down," "Shush, shush," or "Stop it!" A child hardly ever hears such orders. When Elliot's father tells him to calm down, Elliot doesn't hear him; it doesn't help the situation! Great joy needs to be expressed, so allow the child to get it out before helping the child to settle down. Only then you can deal with the child about the situation at hand.

54

• Reflect.

Reflect with the child about how to consider the feelings of others when sharing joy with them. You can do this by asking some questions:

➜ How might your joy affect your friends?

➜ How will your friend going through a hard time feel about your joy?

➜ Could your joy make it harder for your friend to face his own difficulties?

➜ How could you be tactful out of consideration for your friend?

True joy makes us happy and others happy too!

TEACH BY EXAMPLE

As an adult, I feel joy too: when I make a big effort and succeed; when I hear some good news; when my eldest daughter passes her exam; when I'm praised at work...

When I'm bursting with joy, do I take the time to think of others? Or do I impose it on those around me, tactlessly or thoughtlessly?

Do I explain to my child why I didn't shout for joy when he won a judo medal just after his friend had failed? Do I share why I didn't brag to my neighbor about my joy to be off on a skiing holiday when she can't afford a vacation?

Printed in June 2022, by Dimograf, Poland
Job number MGN22020
Printed in compliance with the Consumer Protection Safety Act, 2008